MW01241219

Sri Guru Gobind Singh Jee

A Short Biography

Harjinder Singh

Copyright © Harjinder Singh 2017

All rights reserved.

No part of this publication may be reproduced, stored in an information storage and retrieval system, or transmitted in any form or by any means, electronic, mechanical, photocopying, recording or otherwise without written permission of Akaal Publishers.

First Published by Akaal Publishers in 2017

British Library Cataloguing in Publication Data
A catalogue record for this book is available from the British Library

ISBN 978-0-9554587-8-1

Cover Image by Harjinder Singh Sunner
Cover Design by Harvir Singh
Insides Image also by Harjinder Singh Sunner

Akaal Publishers is a not for profit publisher which publishes books with timeless messages, based upon Sikh history, ethics and philosophy.

For further information see our website:
www.akaalpublishers.com
All rights reserved.

DEDICATION

Dedicated to the Father of the Khalsa,
Sri Guru Gobind Singh Jee

All victories belong to the wonderful enlightener

Introductory Note

In this book I have kept to trying being as respectful to the Gurus as I would be in normal everyday life. So the respectful terms of 'Sri' which means supreme, maybe added to the titles of Sikh Gurus throughout the book when I write about them. Another respectful term is that of 'Jee' which is used at the end of names in the book – again this denotes respect for the person mentioned like adding Bsc, Msc, Phd may do for those with these honorific titles. 'Sahib' which means master may also be added to peoples' names or names of geographical locations. The word 'Sahibzada' refers to 'a son of the master' so a son of Sri Guru Gobind Singh Jee – the Sahibzadas are the four sons of the Guru. Sometimes the term 'Sahibzade' is used it is plural for 'Sahibzada.' They are also conferred with the title of 'Baba' at times which means respected elder.

I have not added a glossary of terms but with the above in mind and my explanations and translations throughout, readers should be able to get through the book with ease, even if they have no prior knowledge of the Punjabi language.

Finally the word 'Guru' translates to one who enlightens with spiritual wisdom.

Harjinder Singh

CONTENTS

ACKNOWLEDGEMENTS

I am indebted first and foremost to Sri Guru Gobind Singh Jee – the tenth Sikh Guru, whose amazing inspirational life will fill the forthcoming pages. This book is a short synopsis of this philosopher, poet, warrior and spiritual master's short life (1666 – 1708 CE). Writings of this Guru extraordinaire are quoted throughout from 'Dasam Granth' – the tenth Guru's anthology.

The main source of research for the book has been Dr Bhai Vir Singh's 'Kalgidhar Chamatkar' secondary sources were from open source data available on the internet. Some of the history that I have written about was of second nature to me, learnt over the years from listening to many oral narrations of Sikh History from the writings of Bhai Santokh Singh in his exegesis of Sikh History the 'Sooraj Parkash' and from reading many books over the years as a Sikh myself.

Most of the content herein has been published by Akaal Publishers on social media and is represented here in an edited format. The content was posted under the hashtag *#350YrsDasmeshPita* to coincide with the 350th Birth anniversary of Sri Guru Gobind Singh Jee which was celebrated this year in Bihar, India at Sri Patna Sahib. To find images associated with the history of this book you are advised to search the hashtag and you will find an array of images.

I would like to thank my team at Akaal Publishers for all their ongoing support and dedication – Amerdip Kaur, Harvir Singh, Upjeet Kaur, Rajvinder Kaur, Baljinder Kaur and Harkaran Singh without them this publication would not have been possible. I apologise for any inaccuracies or errors in the forthcoming pages they are solely mine and readers can email me on **info@akaalpublishers.com** for any feedback.

Harjinder Singh
8.12.17

1 SRI HEMKUNT SAHIB

'Bachittar Natak' translated becomes 'the wonderful story' it is the autobiography of Sri Guru Gobind Singh Jee (1666 – 1708 CE), in it the Guru describes how he meditated at Hemkunt Sahib in his previous life. It is now a Sikh Gurdwara in the Himalayan region. The Guru describes his meditations there in the following way:

"Now I relate my own story as to how I was brought here (as Guru Gobind Singh), while I was absorbed in deep meditation. The site (of my meditation) was the mountain named Hemkunt, (surrounded) with seven peaks and looks very impressive.1.

That mountain is called Sapt Shring (seven-peaked mountain), where the King Pandu (Father of the Pandavas of the Mahabharat) practiced Yoga (austerities). There I was absorbed in deep meditation on the Primal Power, the Supreme God of all time (Mahakal).2.

In this way, my meditation reached its zenith and I became One with the Omnipotent Lord. My parents also meditated for the union with the Incomprehensible Lord and performed many types of disciplines for union.3.

The service that they rendered the Incomprehensible Lord, caused the pleasure of the Supreme Guru (i.e. Lord). When the Lord ordered me, I was born in this Iron age (Kaljug – the present era).4.

I had no desire to come (to the world), because I was totally absorbed in devotion for the Holy feet of the Lord (in a meditative state – smadhi)..." (Dasam Granth, 132)

So Sri Guru Gobind Singh Jee in a previous life meditated and became one with God at this site of Hemkunt Sahib which is now a site of pilgrimage for many Sikhs and non-Sikhs. It was the meditations that took place here that led to the revelation of Sri Guru Gobind Singh Jee into world history, the Guru narrates this himself above. Visiting and traversing the mountain valleys to visit Hemkunt Sahib is breathtaking due to the beauty of the region.

The Gurdwara is open only a few months a year, usually from April/May – September due to the cold weather associated with the peak. The cold weather at the peak adds to the inspiration of the shrine as does the lack of oxygen – the Guru sat and meditated here in isolation and under threat from the elements. This was done to lessen the meditations needed by future aspirants to reach God. The Guru shared his divinity through gracefully liberating others and instructing them onto the right path as instructed by God.

Hemkunt Sahib has a lake which pilgrims bathe in and it is surrounded by seven peaks. The seven peaks have Nishan Sahibs – the Sikh flag installed – the flag is changed on an annual basis at each peak by a group of expert climbers.

2 CONCEPTION

The conception of Sri Guru Gobind Singh Jee took place at the modern day city of Allahabad, India. The first ever 'Sri Akhand Paath Sahib' which is a continuous reading of what was then known as Sri Aad Granth Sahib – the primal Sikh Scripture was completed here. The recital was held in order for the conception of Sri Guru Gobind Singh Jee to take place. The parents of Sri Guru Gobind Singh Jee, his father the ninth Sikh Guru – Sri Guru Tegh Bahadur Jee (1621 – 1675 CE) and Mata (mother) Gujari Jee arranged this recital. Sri Guru Gobind Singh Jee describes this in Bachittar Natak in the following way:

"My father (Sri Guru Tegh Bahadur Jee) proceeded towards the east and visited several places of pilgrimage (preaching about Sikhi on the way – this is after leaving Punjab). When he went to Triveni (Prayag – modern day, Allahabad), he passed his days in acts of charity.1. I was conceived there (at Allahabad) and took birth at Patna." (Sri Dasam Granth, 142/3)

Sri Guru Tegh Bahadur Jee after travelling and preaching Sikhi, decided to stay 6 months at Allahabad. Many prominent Sikhs accompanied the ninth Guru, as did their mother, Mata Nanaki Jee, & Mata Gujari Jee their wife. Mata Nanaki Jee supplicated to their son Sri Guru Tegh Bahadur Jee that he should fulfill her desire of seeing a grandchild, before she passes away, as she was now elderly. Sri Guru Tegh Bahadur Jee accepted his mother's wishes and performed the first ever Sri Akhand Paath at what is now called 'Pakki Sangat Gurdwara' in Allahabad. In this Sri Akhand Paath the following Sikhs recited the scriptures, Bhai Matidas Jee, Bhai Satidas Jee, Bhai Gurbaksh Singh Jee Masand, Bhai Dyala Jee, Baba Gurditta Jee (a descendant of Baba Budhha Jee). This Sri Akhand Paath was done with an 'Akhand Jaap of Sri Japji Sahib'(continuous recital of the first Sikh prayer) too and the Pakki Sangat Gurdwara has continued this tradition of conducting Sri Akhand Paaths in the same manner to the present day.

3 SRI PATNA SAHIB

Patna is the capital of the Indian state of Bihar, it is situated in the East of India. It was here that Sri Guru Gobind Singh Jee was born and the site is now referred to 'Patna Sahib' with its own train station and attracting many a pilgrim.

The beginning of Sikh History associated with Patna starts with Sri Guru Nanak Dev Jee (1469 – 1539 AD) the first Sikh Guru visiting the house of Salas Rai Jauri there. Bhai Mardana Jee an associate of Sri Guru Nanak was sent to get a gem valued by Salas Rai who responded by saying the gem is priceless and requested to meet the owner of the jewel. Salas Rai was inspired by Sri Guru Nanak and converted his home into a Dharamsala (place of worship). Guru Jee blessed Salas Rai with many boons and said his family would be the custodians of this Dharamsala for generations to come.

It was in this house of Salas Rai that Sri Guru Tegh Bahadur Jee later came to and got Mata Nanaki Jee and Mata Gurjari to stay at, when he moved onto preach in the Eastern extremities of India in Assam etc. This house is what is now known as Takhat Sri Harimander Jee (the temple of God), Patna Sahib – where Sri Guru Gobind Singh Jee was born.

The child 'Gobind Rai' was born in the South Asian month of 'Poh'(December/January) in 1666AD. Gobind Rai was the name of Sri Guru Gobind Singh Jee before he was anointed the tenth Guru of the Sikhs.

Pir Bhikhan Shah was a gifted Muslim Saint who lived in modern day Haryana, he had visions of the birth of 'Gobind Rai' and immediately made his way to Patna to have a blessed glimpse (Darshan) of the divine baby. Dr Bhai Vir Singh in his book 'Kalghidhar Chamatkar' gives the following account of what transpired (accounts differ hence why I have provided the source). Pir Bhikhan Shah asked for an audience with the baby 'Gobind Rai' and he cradled him. The Pir then thought, 'who will you favour (Hindus or Muslims)?' He wanted to know the answer to this question so he got two utensils and put milk in one and water in the other and then placed these before the baby Gobind Rai. Gobind Rai placed his baby hands on both utensils and spilt them. The water and milk spilt and mixed together.

Even as an infant Gobind Rai was recognised as the divine light of God manifested in human form, by spiritualists like Pir Bhikan Shah and their doubts were dispelled by him. The spilling and mixing of the water signified the recognition of God in all and making one and all recognise that light of God. Sri Guru Gobind Singh Jee has extensively written about this philosophy in his prayer 'Akaal Ustat' which praises God:

Someone is Hindu and someone a Muslim, then someone is Shia, and someone a Sunni, but all the human beings, as a species, are recognized as one and the same. (Sri Dasam Granth, 51)

This child Gobind Rai would go on to unify righteous people, spreading divine wisdom as he travelled and fight tyrannical rule of marauding invaders and Emperors which plagued the South Asian peninsula.

I was conceived there (Allahabad) and took birth at Patna.
(Sri Dasam Granth, 143)

4 THE MISSION

What was the mission of Sri Guru Gobind Singh Jee? Why was he sent to earth by God to enlighten us? A summary of this mission is given in Bachittar Natak:

Those who mediated on the Name of the Lord, no sorrows and sins came near them. Those who meditated on any other entity (other than God), they ended themselves in futile debates and quarrels.41.

I have been sent into this world by the Preceptor-Lord to propagate Dharma (righteousness). The Lord asked me to spread Dharma, and vanquish the tyrants and evil-minded persons. 42.

I have taken birth for this purpose, all saints should understand this (as my mission). (I have been born) to spread Dharma, and protect saints, and root out all tyrants and evil-minded persons.43. (Sri Dasam Granth, 138)

The mission of Sri Guru Gobind Singh Jee was to nurture saints and protect them. An ideal man of a saint and soldier would emerge through this profound mission. Sikhi (the faith of the Sikhs) would be made eternal in the process.

In the above verses the Guru repeatedly states that his mission is to instill 'Dharma' & uproot tyranny. 'Dharma' is one of those words which cannot be translated into the English language effectively as it is very wide in interpretation. We usually state 'Dharma' as 'righteous living' but it encapsulates Gurbani (scriptures of the

Gurus), Rehat (daily living) and history. So it means to live a life which is virtuous, knowledgeable, and based on the divine wisdom of Gurbani, ethical History and spiritually led. I have tried my best to describe and define 'Dharma' but it is far wider than what I can describe in words.

The second point repeatedly made in the above quotation, is to 'uproot tyranny' – this is the 'Dharma' of the Khalsa (initiated Sikhs or the pure), to be peaceful and draw the sword to uphold and maintain peace against tyrants. This beautiful nature of the Khalsa and the Guru will be elaborated upon in the coming chapters.

I have been sent into this world by the Preceptor-Lord to propagate Dharma (righteousness). The Lord asked me to spread Dharma, and vanquish tyrants & the evil

(Sri Dasam Granth, 138)

5 MARTIAL TRAINING

The maternal uncle or 'Mama' of Sri Guru Gobind Singh Jee was Kirpal Chand Jee he taught the child Gobind Rai how to use a bow and arrow. Kirpal Chand Jee was the brother of Mata Gujari Jee and he was a central figure in the whole life of Sri Guru Gobind Singh Jee. Kirpal Chand Jee was in the army of the seventh Sikh Guru - Sri Guru Har Rai Jee. He regularly visited Sri Guru Tegh Bahadur Jee when he was living at Baba Bakala (before being appointed the Guru). He was the guardian and advisor of Sri Guru Gobind Singh Jee for many years.

At Patna Sahib he educated the child Gobind Rai and acted as his guardian in the absence of Sri Guru Tegh Bahadur Jee who did not return to Patna for many years and remained on his missionary tours. He trained the young 'Gobind Rai' in martial arts. 'Gobind Rai' used these skills to train his friends and engage in mock battles to prepare for the future. During these younger years, 'Gobind Rai' was often referred to as 'Bala Pritam' (Beloved child) and a great number of inspirational stories exist about Bala Pritam, some of which will now be shared in the coming chapters.

Kirpal Chand Jee later accompanied Guru Sahib's family to Anandpur Sahib from Patna Sahib. He fought in the first battle of Sri Guru Gobind Singh at Bhangaani (near the modern day Paonta Sahib) and Guru Sahib praised his valour. He outlived Sri Guru Gobind Singh Jee and conducted Seva (voluntary service) of Gurdwaras at Amritsar towards the end of his life. (source: http://www.thesikhencyclopedia.com)

6 CHILDHOOD & QUEEN MAINI

Gurudwara Baal Lila Maini (Maini Sangat), PATNA (Bihar) is in a narrow lane close to Takht Patna Sahib. It marks the house where Raja (king) Fateh Chand Maini lived with his wife Rani (Queen) Vishwambar Devi Maini (referred to as Rani Maini henceforth). The Gurdwara is called 'Baal Lila' as it refers to acts of inspiration by Gobind Rai as a 'Baal' or child, 'Lila' translates to acts of play.

The Maini King and Queen were childless but very devout and spiritual. Gobind Rai started to frequent the house of the couple. He would come with his friends on a daily basis and eat spiced grams (kale sholle) at their home. The couple started devoting more and more time to meditation after getting the sangat (company) of 'Gobind Rai' and they desired a child.

The Rani Maini made a supplication to 'Gobind Rai' that she wished for a child like him to be born to her and 'Gobind Rai' said, 'there can only be one like me – accept me as your own son'. Rani Maini was overwhelmed with joy with his answer and the couple treated 'Gobind Rai'as their own child from that day forth and served him and his friends with much devotion. 'Gobind Rai' would also address the Rani as 'Ma' (mother).

'Gobind Rai' went to the house of Rani Maini on a daily basis until he left Patna for Punjab. The Gurdwara now serves spiced grams (kale sholle) as parshad (blessed food) to anyone who visits the Gurdawa in memory of Guru Sahib. Historical items that can be viewed at the Gurdwara are an old painting of the child 'Gobind Rai,' his shoes, his Katar (a weapon) & a Sri Guru Granth Sahib Jee that is signed by Guru Jee (these things were previously listed on the history board of the Gurdwara, before it's renovation). Unfortunately, much of the old (antique architecture) structure has been renovated. Previously the

9

Gurdwara had the charm of a comfortable home and one could imagine Gobind Rai entering with his friends and being entertained by Rani Maini and her husband. The current structure of the Gurdwara has lost this charm with its renovation but one can still view historical artefacts and take inspiration and solace from visiting the Gurdwara.

'Gobind Rai' said, 'there can only be one like me – accept me as your own son'

7 KANHGHAN GHAT

Gurdwara Kangan Ghat (Gobind Ghat) is situated on the bank of the river Ganga (Ganjes) and is hardly 200 yards from Takhat Sri Harimandir Jee Patna Sahib. The young Gobind Rai used to play here with his friends, the river Ganga used to flow here before, so this was the river bank – the river has now receded further out from this site and can be reached via a short walk.

It was here that a Hindu priest Pandit Shiv Datt used to meditate, he was a follower of Ram Chandar, the Hindu Prophet. Pandit Shiv Datt quickly realised that Gobind Rai was the image of God and he used to get insights into spirituality from him, through conversations they held.

One day, when playing near the river, Gobind Rai lost one of his gold bangles (kanghan) in the river. When he returned home his friends told Mata Gujari Jee that he had lost a gold bracelet in the river. Mata Jee returned to the river with Gobind Rai and asked 'Where did you lose the gold bracelet?' Gobind Rai threw the other gold bracelet (kanghan) he was wearing in to the river and said 'That's where I lost the other one.' Everyone was shocked that he had now thrown the second bracelet into the river. Even at a young age Gobind Rai had no attachment to the false wealth and riches of the world.

Some historians argue it was an iron bracelet that was thrown into the river, but gold bracelets are mentioned more often historically.

8 MEETING SRI GURU TEGH BAHADUR JEE

Sri Guru Tegh Bahadur Jee carried on with his preaching tour of Sikhi in what is today East India and Bangladesh, visiting many centres where Sri Guru Nanak Dev Jee had previously planted the seeds of Sikhi. Guru Sahib did this extensively for over 4 years.

The first meeting of Gobind Rai with his father – Sri Guru Tegh Bahadur Jee, thus occurred at what is today Gurdwara Guru Ka Bagh (the garden of the Guru) which is situated in Patna City Dhaulpura area (about 3km from Patna Sahib Gurdwara). The tree under which Guru Sahib sat has been preserved.

Gobind Rai came out to this garden along with many Sikhs of Patna. The garden was owned by Rahim Baksh & Karim Baksh. The garden was lifeless and withering but with the arrival of Sri Guru Tegh Bahadur Jee it instantly and miraculously turned lush and green. The owners of the garden heard about this miracle and donated the garden to the Guru. The owners' families had faith in Guru Nanak from generations and were delighted that Guru Sahib had graced their barren garden and made it prosperous.
Gobind Rai (aged 4 years old) bowed to Sri Guru Tegh Bahadur Jee upon meeting him and the family returned to what is now Takhat Sri Harmandir Jee, Patna Sahib which had become their home.

Sri Guru Tegh Bahadur Jee left Patna Sahib quite quickly, they left to go to Anandpur Sahib (then known as Chak Nanaki), Punjab. For the trip they took many Sikhs with them but did not take their family. The family were instructed to wait at Patna Sahib until the Guru had arrived at Anandpur Sahib and then to leave Patna Sahib when instructed. After Sri Guru Tegh Bahadur Jee had been residing at Anandpur Sahib for 4 months they sent a message to their family at Patna Sahib, to now make their journey to Anandpur Sahib too.

9 LEAVING PATNA & HANDI SAHIB

The Sikhs and local people of Patna Sahib had come to adore the inspirational, spiritual and mischievous nature of the child Gobind Rai. From the time of his birth and to the age of 4 years old – he had advised many on spirituality, he had inspired many with his miraculous ways. He had been mischievous when playing with his friends, breaking pots, shooting arrows and practising warfare – but how were the locals to know that these acts were all done to prepare for greater battles in later life.

Each time people had their pots broken or goods damaged by Gobind Rai and his friends, Mata Gujari Jee would compensate those whose goods had been damaged, with money in excess of the value of their items. But now with the imminent departure of Gobind Rai even those who had been upset at times with the child, were now sad that they would miss him.

Due to the distress of separation of Gobind Rai, Mama Kirpal Chand, Mata Gujari and Mata Nanaki, the congregation of Patna started to walk with them to see them off from Patna Sahib. They walked for many kilometres like this not realising the distance walked and could not commit to seeing the family off. They arrived at Danapur and visited the house of an old lady who served a 'handi' (rice and lentils) to the visiting congregation. She had only a small amount of 'Handi' cooked and she was scared that it would run out and not fulfil the whole congregation for their evening meal.

Gobind Rai advised the lady to keep the pot covered and meditate whilst serving the Handi and in this way the Handi did not run out. This building was converted into a Dharmsala and today is known as Gurdwara Handi Sahib, a boon was also given that 'Handi' would always be served as parshad (blessed offering) to those visiting. To this day when you visit, you will be blessed with a small portion of Handi to eat when visiting.

It was here that the final send off of Gobind Rai and his family was conducted by the devotees of Patna. They watched with anguish as the caravan of the Gurus' family disappeared into the distance. They had had four blissful years in the presence of Gobind Rai and the Gurus' family. They had lost their easy access to spiritual upliftment and guidance, and would now have to travel north to Punjab to meet Gobind Rai and his family.

The emotions of the congregation being separated from Gobind Rai can be summed up in the imagery that Sri Guru Amar Das Jee creates here in his Shabad,

Each and every instant,
the rainbird cries and calls.
Without seeing her Beloved,
she does not sleep at all.
She cannot endure this separation.
When she meets the True Guru, then
she intuitively meets her Beloved.

(Sri Guru Granth Sahib Jee, 1262)

10 LAKHNAUR SAHIB

On their journey to Anandpur Sahib (then known as Chak Nanaki) - one of the places that Sri Guru Gobind Singh Jee stopped at was his maternal grandparents village (his Nanake). So this village known as 'Lakhnaur' was the village of Mama Kirpal Chand. It is now known as Lakhnaur Sahib and is part of Ambala, Haryana. It can be reached via roads connecting to Ambala from the Grand Trunk Road or Highway 1 as it is referred to today.

The family stayed here for at least a few weeks before departing onwards to Anandpur Sahib (historical accounts differ on the amount of time spent here). Once again the local population were in awe of the blessed, inspirational and spiritually gifted child that would become 'Sri Guru Gobind Singh Jee'. The locals were full of detachment and sadness when the family were about to leave.

Some historical artefacts are maintained at the Gurdwara they are:

- Two teer (arrows) of Sri Guru Gobind Singh Jee

- The manjia (beds) of Sri Guru Gobind Singh Jee & Mata Gujari Jee

- A shield of Sri Guru Gobind Singh Jee & two cauldrons (praata) of Mata Gujari Jee

11 FATHERS' MARTYRDOM

The Mughal Ruler Aurangzeb (1618 – 1707 CE) was evil, fanatical and tyrannical. He had murdered his brothers and imprisoned his father to become the Emperor of the Mughal Rule (kingdom) – which at that time included Punjab and areas where Sikhs resided.

The Sikhs had been peaceful with the Mughals until the fifth Sikh Guru - Sri Guru Arjan Dev Jee (1563 – 1605 CE), was martyred after undergoing inhumane tortures. The Gurus' torture was conducted with the explicit permission of the then Mughal Emperor Jahangir (1569 – 1627 CE). This martyrdom changed the Sikhs policy of defence from only peaceful means to now drawing swords, when all peaceful means had been exhausted. So, the Sixth Guru, Sri Guru Har Gobind Sahib (1596 – 1638 CE), did now actually engage in military conflicts with the Mughals and led an army.

The Sikhs now started following the philosophy of being saints and warriors, carrying rosaries and swords. The Sikhs now would emulate meditation of the rosary and sword. Weapons would be revered and worshipped. Arms would be used to quell tyranny, whilst the rosary would ensure a humane soldier emerged who was forever watchful and disciplined, one that did not exploit power that the sword would wield.

The Emperor Aurangzeb was imposing taxes upon non-Muslims and trying to convert the population en masse to Islam. Many things were done by him to make life testing for any non Muslims – thus those of other faiths were under pressure of becoming completely assimilated.

It needs to be made clear that 'Sikhs' who lived with the Guru or in municipalities set up by the Gurus did not fall foul to the conversion tactics of Aurangzeb, as much as the general population. This was due to the fact that the Guru's purchased land and founded their own cities and/or de facto kingdoms which were ruled predominantly by the edicts of the Gurus.

With this pressure building upon Hindu populations some Kashmiri Pandits (Hindu priests) took a delegation to Sri Guru Tegh Bahadur Jee with a supplication to protect their religious freedom. Kirpa Raam led this delegation and humbly supplicated that they were now completely at the mercy of the Guru to protect them and no other could now save their impending assimilation into Islam.

Sri Guru Tegh Bahadur Jee had replied that, 'The sacrifice of a great soul is required to protect these religious freedoms.' At this point his son, 'Gobind Rai' had said, 'Father there is no one greater than you.' So it was Sri Guru Gobind Singh Jee who had suggested the sacrifice of his own father, Sri Guru Tegh Bahadur Jee. Thus, Sri Guru Tegh Bahadur Jee sent a message to Aurangzeb that all Hindus would convert to Islam if he could get him to covert (Guru Sahib to convert). Thus, Aurangzeb asked for Sri Guru Tegh Bahadur Jee to come to Delhi for an audience. Aurangzeb could not convert Guru Sahib even after torturing his close confidants to death (Bhai Mati Das, Bhai Sati Das, Bhai Deyala) and in turn martyred Guru Sahib by ordering an execution (beheading) in Chandni Chowk Delhi. Today Gurdwara Sees Ganj Sahib marks the site of martyrdom of Sri Guru Tegh Bahadur Jee and opposite is the place where the Sikhs of the Guru were tortured to death, sawn in half, boiled alive and burnt alive. Rakab Ganj Gurdwara in Delhi marks the site of cremation of the body of Sri Guru Tegh Bahadur Sahib Jee.

Sri Guru Gobind Singh Jee writes about the sacrifice of his father in his Bachittar Natak in the following way:

He protected the forehead mark and sacred thread (of the Hindus) which marked a great event in the Iron age (of Kaljug).

17

For the sake of saints, he laid down his head without any remorse.13.

For the sake of Dharma, he sacrificed himself. He laid down his head but not his creed (meaning he did not forsake his principles).

The saints of the Lord abhor the performance of miracles and malpractices. (Aurangzeb had asked the Guru to prove his spirituality by performing a miracle and he could then be pardoned, which the Guru refused to do). *14.*

Breaking the pot of his body as ordered by the head of Delhi (Aurangzeb), He left for the abode of the Lord. None could perform such a feat as that of Tegh Bahadur.15.

The whole world bemoaned the departure of Tegh Bahadur. What the world lamented, was hailed in the heavens – with his arrival.16. (Sri Dasam Granth, 131)

He protected the forehead mark and sacred thread (of the hindus)... For the sake of dharma, he sacrificed himself.

(Sri Dasam Granth, 131)

12 CREMATION AT ANANDPUR SAHIB

Bhai Jaita Jee had been told by Sri Guru Tegh Bahadur Jee that he was to take his beheaded head to Anandpur Sahib after his execution in Delhi. Baba Gurditta Jee (a descendant of Baba Buddha Jee) was also given a coconut, money and offerings that would confer the Guruship to his son 'Gobind Rai.' Baba Gurditta Jee had immediately left Delhi to confer the Guruship onto 'Gobind Rai' when ordered by Sri Guru Tegh Bahadur Jee, prior to the execution. Whereas Bhai Jaita Jee had to wait and witness the martyrdom   of Sri Guru Tegh Bahadur Jee and the merciless torturing to death of his fellow Sikhs, Bhai Mati Das, Bhai Sati Das and Bhai Dayala.

As soon as Sri Guru Tegh Bahadur Jee was beheaded the 'head' of Guru Sahib was transported by Bhai Jaita Jee. Accounts differ of the 'head' miraculously falling into Bhai Jaita Jee's lap and/or Bhai Jaita Jee simply recovering the head as a storm had suddenly broken and confusion had ensued after the execution.

After an arduous and treacherous journey of 5 days Bhai Jaita Jee arrived at Kiratpur Sahib from Delhi. This journey would have been approximately 350km and Bhai Jaita Jee had to travel through jungles, forests and unconventional routes as he was secretly carrying the head of the Guru. The imperial forces could not catch him doing this – so he ran most of the way and used any means he could, to get to Kiratpur Sahib without being detected. This tallies to about 70km travel a day – a truly herculean effort.

Messages were sent to Anandpur Sahib to Guru Gobind Rai and the Sikhs to come and have sight of the head of the Guru. Where Bhai Jaita Jee presented the 'head' of Sri Guru Tegh Bahadur Jee to Sri Guru Gobind Singh Jee today stands Gurdwara Bibangarh Sahib, Kiratpur. From Kiratpur Sahib the 'head' was respectfully carried on a palanquin to Anandpur Sahib. Here, the cremation of the head was discussed and Mata Gujari Jee had said the head should be cremated in Anandpur Sahib as the city was founded by Sri Guru Tegh Bahadur Jee. So the cremation took place at what is now known as Gurdwara Sis Ganj Sahib, Anandpur, the ashes were also buried here at the same site. Sri Guru Gobind Singh Jee built the platform over the ashes himself.

The reign of being the tenth Guru began with the young Guru Gobind Rai cremating the head of his father. This event signalled the reigniting of military activity of Sikhs. After the martyrdom of the fifth Guru – Sri Guru Arjan Dev Jee his son the sixth Guru – Sri Guru HarGobind Sahib Jee had defended himself and the Sikhs by raising an army and entering combat if and when pressed to. Now, after a peaceful period of the seventh, eighth and ninth Gurus in which no battles were entertained - Guru Gobind Rai would start entering battles when peaceful means had been exhausted. He would shape the identity of Sikhs permanently and leave a lasting inspiration in the annals of history of political diplomacy, sovereignty and battle heroics against all the odds.

The whole world bemoaned the departure of Tegh Bahadur. What the world lamented, was hailed in the heavens – with his arrival.
(Sri Dasam Granth, 131)

20

13 ANANDPUR SAHIB - THE ABODE OF BLISS

Anandpur – Anand translates to meaning bliss. 'Pur' translates to meaning abode, more commonly in this class referring to a township. The word 'Sahib' means master and is attached to the name of the township as a mark of respect so Sikhs will be heard calling the geographical location 'Anandpur Sahib.'

Anandpur Sahib was the Sikh kingdom founded by Sri Guru Tegh Bahadur Jee and ruled over and defended by Sri Guru Gobind Singh Jee. Sri Guru Tegh Bahadur Jee had purchased the land and founded the city, it was initially referred to as 'Chak Nanaki' after the mother of Sri Guru Tegh Bahadur Jee – Mata Nanaki.

Anandpur Sahib was a fully functional independent state. Sri Guru Gobind Singh set up commerce, industry and farming, inviting traders and Sikhs to settle here – it was the capital city of the Sikhs for some years. It's green hilly lands, tranquil surrounds and proximity to the Sirsa River made it both peaceful and defendable against invaders and offensive forces.

Sri Guru Gobind Singh Jee led the Sikh community from here and inspired the masses with his spiritual prowess and statesmanship. He was a poet, a warrior and one endowed with divine wisdom. Five forts were constructed over a ten year period in Anandpur Sahib, they were all strategically linked by underground tunnels and roads. These forts would become central to the defence of Anandpur Sahib:

1) Anandgarh – fort of bliss – the biggest fort and with the best defences – it still stands and can be seen today. Although much of the original fort is now underground and inaccessible.

2) Lohgarh – for of iron. An arms factory and depository

3) Holgarh – where war games of Holla Mohalla took place

4) Fatehgarh – named after the youngest son of Sri Guru Gobind Singh Jee, Sahibzada Baba Fateh Singh Jee

5) Taragarh/Agamgarh – fort of stars/peace. This fort is known by two names that of stars and peace. Many meditative Sikhs lived here on the outskirts of Anandpur Sahib in tranquillity. It was also a watch point – to spy on entrants into Anandpur Sahib. Even today very few Sikhs or pilgrims, visit the site of this fort and it remains very tranquil.

The sixth fort 'Kesgarh Sahib' – fort of unshorn hair called 'Kes' was a point for mass gatherings upon a hill. From historical records it seems probable that this fort/Gurdwara which is now the most famous in Anandpur Sahib was actually constructed after the initiation ceremony of the Khalsa which took place here. So rather than being a fort in the times of the Guru it was a site to hold large congregations at Anandpur Sahib.

14 REVELATION OF THE KHALSA - VAISAKHI

Vaisakhi is the first day of the month 'Vaisakh' which falls between April and May. The day of Vaisakhi is usually on the 13th or 14th of April – the dates change each year in line with lunar movements.

The Vaisakhi of 1699 CE marked the pinnacle of a 300 year evolution of the Sikh spirit, philosophy & discipline. A new initiation ceremony was established in which five Sikhs called 'Panj Pyare' (the five beloved ones) would preside over the ceremony and prepare the initiation of 'Amrit' meaning 'nectar of immortality' by reciting five prayers and stirring a 'Khanda' (double-edged sword) in an iron vessel that has water and 'patase' (glucose and sugar puffs) in it. By creating the Amrit via the Khanda, the Guru imbued the sweetness of peace and humility into his Sikhs, alongside a ferocious and indomitable warrior spirit. The sweetness came from the patase and prayers of peace, the warrior spirit came from being reborn from a pure iron vessel and from the tip of the double-edged sword. The Guru also authored many a verse that imbued the warrior spirit.

After the completion of the fortifications of Anandpur Sahib which took 10 years, the Guru then created the nation of the 'Khalsa' (the pure). Sikhs who were now initiated, were referred to as Khalsa and had to follow a discipline which included a uniform of five articles of faith. These articles of faith are sometimes referred to as the '5 Ks' they are to be worn at all times and never removed from the body. They are keeping unshorn hair (Kes), wearing a Kascherra (a specially designed underwear), wearing an iron bangle (kara) upon your wrist, kirpan (sword of mercy, usually a dagger size nowadays), Kangha a wooden comb kept in the Kes. The Kes would be complemented with a turban giving the Khalsa a distinct identity. The Khalsa has to recite a minimm of 7 daily prayers (Japji Sahib, Jaap Sahib, Svaye, Choupai Sahib, Anand Sahib, Rehras Sahib & Kirtan Sohila).

The Khalsa has to refrain from all sin, living a saintly life. Severe sins for which one would become an apostate and would have to atone and become reinitiated were now defined as:

1) Cutting one's hair, plucking it or dying it.

2) Eating meat, fish or eggs. (Some argue that only Halal meat is outlawed for Sikhs but this only applies to survival situations. So Sikhs are lacto vegetarians and would consume non vegetarian products if they were in a survival situation but even then they would not consume Halal or Kosher meat due to the inhumane method of slaughter.)

3) Taking intoxicants (alcohol or drugs)

4) Having relationships with the opposite sex outside of marriage.

The Khalsa was created as a brotherhood of equals in which each Sikh is a sovereign. All distinctions of caste and familial affiliation are destroyed upon entering the creed of the Khalsa – all males have the surname 'Singh' meaning tiger or lion and females have the surname 'Kaur' which means princess or lioness. The Khalsa have the same Father, Sri Guru Gobind Singh Jee and their mother is Mata Sahib Kaur Jee. Their ancestral village is Anandpur Sahib. They are to be forever loyal to Sikhs and their faith. Should the need arise they will raise arms to defend their faith and Guru. Their life is dedicated to these Khalsa ideals and many more. This is a short synopsis of the Khalsa more can be learnt from other sources such as a book I translated called 'The Sikh Code of Conduct.'

15 SETTLING AT PAONTA SAHIB

The Hindu Hill Raja's (kings of municipalities surrounding Anandpur) were envious of Sri Guru Gobind Singh Jee and the new township of Anandpur Sahib, was in its infancy. The Sikhs had entered skirmishes with the forces of the surrounding kingdoms. At this point the Guru did not want to antagonise the situation and chose to move away to ensure peace was maintained and that no harm came to the residents of Anandpur Sahib. This was done as a strategic tactic to allow the construction and development of Anandpur Sahib to take place without the necessity of having to engage in war. The construction of the forts previously mentioned continued unabated during this period.

The Guru took up the invitation of the Raja of Nahan, Medini Parkash to visit his kingdom. He was one of the local Kings who was hospitable and friendly towards the Guru. The Guru soon took up residence here and Paonta Sahib was established which is in a lush valley of the Himalayan region.

The Guru was at ease here, which allowed him to welcome 52 poets to his court and he engaged in hunting and writing scriptures. Sahibzada Baba Ajit Singh Jee the eldest son of the Guru was born here and major parts of Sri Dasam Granth were authored here, including Jaap Sahib, Svaye and Chandi dee Vaar. These prayers were definitely authored here, but other works were most likely also authored here, but do not get a mention historically.

Pens used by Sri Guru Gobind Singh Jee to write scriptures are still on display at Paonta Sahib today. The 'Kavi Darbar' or court of poets, has been maintained, it was here that poets would present their poetry to the Guru and congregation.

Pir Buddu Shah a Muslim Saint became acquainted with the Guru here. He was inspired and enlightened by the Guru, as were many more. Sri Guru Gobind Singh Jee engaged in his first battle here which took place at Bhangani, which is 6km from Paonta Sahib. Guru Jee prepared for the battle with his forces on a hillock as he knew the Sikhs would be outnumbered by the opposing force of some Hindu kingdoms who had become hostile towards the Guru as they wanted to steal items of wealth from him. Guru Sahib resided here for four years and the battle of Bhangani occurred at the end of the stay, after which the Guru took up residence once more at Anandpur Sahib. Upon arrival at Anandpur Sahib the Guru gave strict orders that those who were unwilling to join the army of the Sikhs must vacate the city – as Guru Sahib knew that battles would now ensue at Anandpur Sahib. Guru Sahib describes this period and the battle of Bhanghani in Bachittar Natak in the following way,

Then I left my home and went to place named Paonta. I enjoyed my stay on the banks of Kalindri (Yamuna) and saw amusement of various kind.2.

There I killed many lions, nilgais (blue bulls) and bears (whilst hunting). On this the king Fateh Shah become angry and fought with me without any reason.3.

BHUJANG PRAYAAT STANZA

There Sri Shah (Sango Shah) become enraged and all the five warriors stood firmly in the battlefield.

(Sango Shah was the commander of the Sikh army for this battle. He along with his four brothers all fought in this battle – these are the five warriors referred to here including Jit Mal, Gulab, Mahari Chand, Ganga Ram. They were all cousins of Guru Sahib, they were the sons of Bibi Veero – the paternal aunt or 'bhooa' of Guru Jee).

Including the tenacious Jit Mal and the hero Gulab, whose faces were red with ire, in the field.4.

26

The persistent Mahari Chand and Ganga Ram, who had defeated a lot of forces. Lal Chand was red with anger, who had shattered pride of several lion-like heroes.5.

Maharu got enraged and with frightening expression killed brave Khans in the battlefield. The godly Daya Ram (first Panj Pyara), filled with great ire, fought very heroically in the field like Dronacharya.6.

Kirpal (Udasi) in rage, rushed with his mace and struck it on the head of the tenacious Hayaat Khan. (The Udasi's followers had deserted the Guru en masse before battle, but their leader Kirpal fought with a mace with much tenacity)

With all his might, he caused the marrow flow out of his head, which splashed like the butter spattering out of the pitcher of butter broken by lord Krishan.7.

Then Nam Chand, in fierce rage, wielding his sword struck it with force. But the sword broke. Then he drew his dagger and the tenacious warrior saved the honour of the Sodhi clan.8.

Then the Maternal uncle Kirpal (Mama Kirpal Chand), in great ire, manifested the war-feats like a true Kshatriya (warrior). The great hero was struck by an arrow, but he caused the brave Khan to fall from the saddle.9.

He slew several graceful warriors, with full force; the soldiers who survived, fled away in order to save their lives.10.

There (Sango) Shah exhibited his acts of bravery in the battlefield and trampled under feet many bloody Khans. Gopal, the king of Guleria, stood firmly in the field and roared like a lion amidst a herd of deers.11.

There in great fury, a warrior Hari Chand, very skillfully took position in the battlefield. He discharged sharp arrows in great rage and whosoever was struck, left for the other world.12.

RASAAVAL STANZA

Hari Chand (Handooria) in great fury, killed significant heroes. He shot skillfully a volley of arrows and killed a lot of forces.13.

He was absorbed in a dreadful feat of arms. Armed warriors were being killed and great kings were falling on the ground.14.

Then Jit Mal aimed and struck Hari Chand down to the ground with his spear.15.

The warriors struck with arrows became red with blood. Their horses fell and they left for heavens.16.

Bhujang Prayaat Chhand

Sahib Chand, the valiant Kshatriya, killed a bloody Khan of Khorasan. In the hands of blood-thirsty Khans, there were the Khorasan swords, whose sharp edges flashed like fire. The bows shooing out volleys of arrows twanged, the splendid horses fell because of the heavy blows.17.

The trumpets sounded and the musical pipes were played, the brave warriors thundered from both sides. And with their strong arms struck (the enemy), the witches drank blood to their fill and produced dreadful sounds.18.

DOHRA
How far should I describe the great battle? Those fought attained martyrdom, thousands fled away. 19.

BHUJANG PRAYAAT STANZA

The hill-chief spurred his horse and fled, the warriors went away without discharging their arrows. The chiefs of Jaswal and Dadhwal, who were fighting (in the field), left with all their soldiers.20.

The Raja of Chandel was perplexed, when the tenacious Hari Chand caught hold of the spear in his hand. He was filled with great fury, fulfilling his duty as a general; those who came in front of him, were cut into pieces and fell (in the field).21.

Then Najabat Khan came forward and struck Sango Shah with his weapons. Several skillful Khans fell on him with their arms and sent Shah Sangram to heaven (Sango Shah attained martyrdom).22.

DOHRA
The brave warrior Sago Shah fell down after killing Najbat Khan. There were lamentations in this world and rejoicing in heaven (due to his death).23.

Bhujang Chhand

When this lowly person saw Shah Sangram falling (while fighting bravely) he held aloft his bow and arrows (Guru Sahib talking about himself and his actions in this war). He, fixing his gaze on a Khan, shot an arrow, which stung the enemy like a black cobra, who (the Khan) fell down.24.

He drew out another arrow and aimed and shot it on the face of Bhikhan Khan. The bloody Khan fled away leaving his horse in the field, who was killed with the third arrow.25.

After regaining consciousness from the swoon, Hari Chand shot his arrows with unerring aim. Whosoever was struck, fell down unconscious, and leaving his body, went to the heavenly abode.26.

He aimed and shot two arrows at the same time and did not care for the selection of his target. Whosoever was struck and pierced by his arrow, went straight to the other world.27.

The warriors remained true to their duty in the field, the witches and ghosts drank blood to their fill and raised shrill voices. The Birs (heroic spirits), Baitals (ghosts) and Siddhs (adepts) laughed, the witches were talking and huge kites were flying (for meat).28.

Hari Chand, filled with rage, drew out his bow, he aimed and shot his arrow, which struck my horse. He aimed and shot the second arrow towards me, the Lord protected me, his arrow only grazed my ear. 29.

His third arrow penetrated deep into the buckle of my waist-belt. Its edge touched the body, but did not cause a wound, the Lord saved his servent.30.

RASAAVAL STANZA

When the edge of the arrow touched my body, it kindled my resentment. I took the bow in my hand and aimed and shot the arrow.31.

All the warriors fled, when a volley of arrow was showered. Then I aimed the arrow on a warrior and killed him.32.

Hari Chand was killed and his brave soldiers were trampled. The chief of Kot Lehar was seized by death.33.

The hill-men fled from the battlefield, all were filled with fear. I gained victory through the favour of the Eternal Lord (KAL).34.

We returned after victory and sang songs of triumph. I showered wealth on the warriors, who were full of rejoicings.35.

(Chapter 8 of Bachittar Natak, Sri Dasam Granth 143 – 149)

Then I left my home and went to place named Paonta. I enjoyed my stay on the banks of Kalindri (Yamuna) and saw amusement of various kind.

(Sri Dasam Granth, 143)

16 BATTLE OF ANANDPUR SAHIB

Sri Guru Gobind Singh Jee had mastered the art of warfare, using varied tactics and strategy in line with the circumstances of the battle being engaged in. Sikhs were always outnumbered in battle. The Mughal ruler Aurangzeb wanted to tax the Hindu Hill Chief kingdoms and Anandpur Sahib which was under the rule of Guru Sahib. Guru Sahib made treaties with the Hill Chiefs and tried to remain on good terms with them. He went as far as urging them to fight the tyranny of the Mughal Rule as he had done by setting up the Khalsa. The Hill Chiefs were disloyal and couldn't keep their word, as they were led by self-interest in maintaining their own states and not upsetting the Mughal emperor. The Hill chiefs preferred servitude to the Mughals rather than defend their kingdoms or oppose the tyranny of the Mughals.

Even though Sri Guru Gobind Singh Jee had helped the Hill Chiefs in battles against the Mughals most of the Hill Chiefs joined forces with the Mughals to oust the Sikhs from Anandpur. This was the final stance taken by these joint forces which had both tasted defeat at the hands of the Guru and his Sikhs. The Mughals and Hill Chiefs were perplexed at the ability of the Sikhs to fight in small numbers. After battles had taken place, more Sikhs would come to Anandpur, and join the Guru's army, thus replenishing those lost in battle.

The final siege of Anandpur saw a joint contingent of about 1 million surround Anandpur in 1704 – made of Mughal forces and Hindu Hill Chiefs armies. Inside Anandpur Sahib it is estimated 10,000 Sikhs resided this may have been accurate for a population figure prior to the final siege and battle of Anandpur. This number would have dwindled prior to the siege and we can only guess that it may have been in the region of 5000 maximum or even just a few thousand then. The opposing armies could not penetrate Anandpur and kept tasting death at each attempt in trying to breach Anandpur. So to stop further losses – they decided to lay siege to Anandpur and hoped to draw out the Sikhs through hunger and desperation. Much to their woe – the siege dragged on for 8 months. The Sikhs inside Anandpur had by now, all gathered at the biggest fort – Anandgarh. The remaining Sikhs were paltry in numbers, many had died of starvation, many had deserted the Guru and now the remaining Sikhs were waiting for the Guru's command to evacuate Anandpur.

The Mughals and Hindu Hill Chiefs had made solemn oaths that no harm would come to the Sikhs if they vacated – but the Guru exposed their lies by sending out carts of rubbish which he had claimed were their valuables and that the Sikhs would follow the safe passage of these carts. These carts were looted by the opposing soldiers posted outside the fort of Anandgarh, breaking their solemn oaths. Yet the Sikhs still wanted to leave due to starvation and the harsh conditions they had been enduring for many months. Thus solemn promises were made once again and the Sikhs vacated Anandgarh. The Sikhs leaving the fort were attacked by the soldiers outside – once again breaking their oaths of safe passage to end the impasse of the siege. Many Sikhs died when leaving the fort and the loss of many rare manuscripts in the Sirsa River occurred at the dead of night when the Sikhs were trying to get out safely from Anandpur Sahib.

Mata Sahib Kaur Jee and Mata Sundar Kaur Jee (wives of the Guru) were sent to Delhi with Bhai Mani Singh. The rest of the family made it to the Sirsa River only to be separated – the younger Sahibzade (two younger sons of the Gur) remained with Mata Gujari Jee their grandmother and the surviving forty Sikhs made it to Chamkaur with the Guru.

17 BRAVE SHAHEEDS OF CHAMKAUR SAHIB

Chamkuar had been previously frequented by the Guru. Upon arrival at Chamkaur, Guru Jee scoured the area for a suitable position to fight from. The 'Chamkaur Dee Garhi' was a building on a hillock, thus it was strategically placed to fight from, for the Sikhs who were short in numbers. Guru Sahib purchased it from its owners and prepared for battle, as the opposing forces were still in pursuit of the Guru and Sikhs.

The following is an extract from my book 'Game of Love.' which details the battle of Chamkaur:

The Sikhs bravely rebuffed the attacks of the opposing forces once again and Sri Guru Gobind Singh Jee reached Chamkaur on the 21 December 1704 after crossing the River Sirsa.

Sri Guru Gobind Singh Jee and forty surviving Sikhs raised a defensive position in a raised mud house (Garhi). The Sikhs showed exemplary bravery in battle from the Chamkaur Garhi, but many of the Sikhs were martyred. Nonetheless Sri Guru Gobind Singh Jee still managed to escape unscathed. In His own words Sri Guru Gobind Singh Jee narrates victory in letters to Aurangzeb the Mughal Emperor. These are called Fatehnama and Zafarnama, meaning prose of victory. Firstly, I will quote the whole of the Fatehnama and provide commentary where necessary:

In the name of the Lord who manifests Himself as weapons of war viz (through) the sword, the axe, the arrow, the spear, and the shield. The Lord is with the brave warriors who, mounted on their horses, fly through the air. The Lord who has bestowed upon you the kingdom (Referring to Aurangzeb), has granted me the honour of protecting the faith. Where as you are engaged in plunder by deceit and lies, I am on the path of truth and purity.

The name "Aurangzeb" does not befit you, since a king who is supposed to bring honour to the throne, will not indulge in deceit

Aurangzeb! Your rosary is nothing more than a bundle of beads and thread. With every move of a bead, you entrap others in your snare Aurangzeb! By your grisly act, you have put your father's name in the dust; by murdering your own brothers, you have added (to the list of your evil deeds) and from that (by imprisoning your father and murdering your brothers) you have laid a weak foundation of your kingdom.

Now by the grace of the Lord, I have made the water of steel (Amrit for my warriors) which will fall upon you like a torrent and with this (torrent of Amrit), your sinister kingdom will vanish from this holy land without a trace. You came thirsty (defeated) from the mountains of South; the Rajputs have also made you drink the bitter cup (of defeat). Now you are casting your sight towards this side (Punjab). Here also your thirst will remain unquenched I will put fire under your feet when you come to Punjab and I will not let you even drink water here. What is so great if a jackal kills two cubs of a tiger by deceit and cunning? (It is unclear if Sri Guru Gobind Singh Jee is referring to his elder or younger sons here, but regardless of this the Sahibzade were all martyred due to treacherous false oaths taken by the Mughals & Hill Rajas in battle.) *Since that formidable tiger (the Khalsa) still lives, he will definitely take revenge (from the jackal - Aurangzeb).*

I no longer trust you or your God since I have seen your God as well as his word. I do not trust your oaths anymore and now there is no other way for me except to take up the sword. (All the battles that Sri Guru Gobind Singh Jee was victorious in were all defensive, in that the Sikhs were attacked and the Sikhs in the times of Sri Gobind Singh Jee never made any territorial land claims even when they were victorious in battle – this is unparralled in history.)

If you are an old fox, I will too keep my tigers out of your snare. If you come to me for detailed and frank talks, I shall show you the path of purity and truthfulness. Let the forces from both sides array in the battlefield at such a distance that they are visible to each other. The battle field should be arranged in such a manner that both the forces should be separated by a reasonable distance (of two furlongs 400metres). Then I will advance in the battle field for combat with your forces along with two of my riders. So far you have been enjoying the fruits of a cosy and comfortable life but never faced the fierce warriors (in the battle field). Now come into the battle field with your weapons and stop tormenting the people who are the creation of the Lord. (Fatehnama, Sri Guru Gobind Singh Jee, translation from www.zafarnama.com)

This challenge from Sri Gobind Singh Jee of an open and face to face battle was never taken up by Aurangzeb. From the wording of the Fatehnama, one can see complete defiance and the spirit of victory of Sri Guru Gobind Singh Jee, even though he had at this time sacrificed his beloved close associates in Chamkaur and his four sons and mother. This is the greatness of the Father of the Sikhs, an undying rising spirit. I will now quote directly from Zafarnama of how Sri Guru Gobind Singh narrates the events of the battle of Chamkaur:

"What can forty hungry men do, when suddenly a 1 million strong army pounces upon them? The promise breakers launched a surprise attack with their swords and arrows and guns. It was out of sheer helplessness that I came in the battle field. (Having thus decided) I came with all the battle plans and munitions.

When the entire stratagem employed for (solving) a problem are exhausted, (only) then taking your hand to the sword is legitimate.

What trust can I have on your oath on Koran? Otherwise you tell why I should have taken this path (of taking up the sword). I do not know that this person (Aurangzeb) is cunning like a fox. Otherwise I would never have come to this place i.e. Chamkaur (by vacating Anandgarh on the false oaths of Aurangzeb and his men). If any person believes an oath on Koran, he should neither be tied (arrested) nor killed.

They (the enemy) dressed in black and like flies came suddenly with great uproar. Any person who came out from behind the wall (at Chamkaur dee garhi), took one arrow (on his body) and was submerged in blood. Any person who did not come out from (behind) that wall, did not take an arrow and (hence) did not become miserable (die, the Sikhs only still attacked those that came forward to attack their battle position and did not kill forces that they could see who were not advancing to Chamkaur dee garhi). When I saw that Nahar had come out from behind the wall for battle, he immediately took one of my arrows on himself (and died).

Many Afghans who used to tell tall stories (about their bravery) also ran away from the battlefield. That large number of other Afghans came for the battle like a flood of arrows and bullets. They launched many a brave attacks. (However) some of these (attacks) were intelligently launched but some were sheer madness. They launched many attacks and they took many wounds upon themselves. They killed two (of my) men and also gave their own lives as well.

That coward Khawaja (who was hiding behind the wall) did not come out in the battlefield like a brave man. Alas! If I had seen his (Khawaja's) face, I would have sent him to the other world just with one arrow.

In the end many fighters from both sides died quickly after being wounded by arrows and bullets. The battlefield was full of (severed) heads and legs, which gave the impression as if these were balls and sticks.

The whizzing of arrows and vibrations of the strings of bows produced huge commotions. And cries of "hai-hu" were coming from the whole battle field. And the dreadful noises of weapons had their affect on the bravest of brave men who gave the impression as if they had lost their mental balance.

And finally what could the bravery of my forty warriors do in battle when countless of these (Afghans) fell upon them." (Zafarnama – verses 19 - 41, Sri Guru Gobind Singh Jee, translation from www.zafarnama.com)

Sri Guru Gobind Singh Jee shows no relenting even though his sons have been sacrificed:

What happened that you have killed four children (my sons); the coiled snake (in the form of my Khalsa) still remains. What manliness you have shown by extinguishing a few sparks (Sahibzadas). You have made the conflagration brighter and more furious.

How nicely the sweet-tongued poet Firdosi has said that "to act in haste is the work of a devil." (Guru Jee is referring to the summary execution of the young Sahibzadas at Sirhind which he has termed as an act of a devil). When I meet you in the court of your Lord, you will appear as a witness there (and answer all the crimes committed by you)." (Zafarnama – verses 78-81, Sri Guru Gobind Singh Jee, translation from www.zafarnama.com)

One final comment on the Chamkaur battle that needs to be noted is that Sri Guru Gobind Singh Jee is a truly a unique Father who could have saved his elder sons from being sacrificed in the battle. Yet, He happily let them enter battle and attain martyrdom. He truly treated all Sikhs as his own children and when leaving the Chamkaur Garhi he took his shoes off so he would not step on any of the martyred Sikhs with his shoes on. This was the love he had for his Sikhs.

Another misconception about the Sikhs and especially the battles of Sri Guru Gobind Singh Jee that needs to be clarified is that the Hindu Hill Rajas were as much against the Sikhs as the Muslim Mughals, sometimes the Islamic element is over-emphasised and the Hindu Hill Rajas are given a convenient oversight. In the Guru's own words,

"I am also the annihilator of the hill rajas, the idol worshippers. They are idol worshipers and I am engaged in defeating "the very concept" of idol worship." (Zafarnama – verse 95, Sri Guru Gobind Singh Jee, translation from www.zafarnama.com)

I would like to also clarify that Sri Guru Gobind Singh Jee fought against tyranny and did not undertake battle to attack any faith or faithful. Sikhs in their zealous nature sometimes refer to the battles of the Guru as being against Muslims, but this is mistaken. The battles were to uproot tyranny regardless of the faith allegiance of those being fought. I think it would also be fitting to quote how Sri Guru Gobind Singh Jee narrates that the faithful are protected by the Almighty in battle and dire circumstances:

"In time of need, He blinds the enemy and takes out the helpless without an injury to him; even from a thorn (a thorn cannot prick him if God does not ordain it). (Guru Jee is referring to his escape from Chamkaur).

The Compassionate Lord always showers mercy upon any person who follows the path of truthfulness. Anyone who serves the Almighty with total devotion is blessed with peace and tranquillity. What deception can an enemy inflict on a person who is under the protection of Lord Himself." (Zafarnama – verses 100-103, Sri Guru Gobind Singh Jee, translation from www.zafarnama.com)

The above lines are universal and apply to the faithful, regardless of their religious allegiance.

I thought it would also be fitting to finish this chapter with the narration of the story of the final martyr of Chamkaur battle – Bibi Harsharan Kaur:

"… in village Khroond, a daughter (Sikh) of Guru Gobind Singh, Bibi Harsharan Kaur, asked for her mother's permission to perform the final rites for the Shaheeds (martyrs of Chamkaur). Her old mother replied, "it is total darkness outside and soldiers are everywhere around the fort, how will you even go near?"

Hearing this, Kalgeedhar's (reference to the plume wearing sovereign – Sri Guru Gobind Singh Jee) lioness daughter replied with resolve "I will avoid the soldiers and perform the cremation, and if need be, I'll fight and die." The mother gave her courage and hugged her daughter and then explained the maryada (rites) to follow for the cremation. After performing Ardas (a prayer of supplication), Bibi Harsharan Kaur left for the Chamkaur Fort.

The battlefield, which saw iron smashing against iron, heard the bellows of elephants, the trotting of hooves and calls of "Kill! Capture!" was now totally silent, and enveloped in complete darkness. In such a situation, the 16 year old girl Bibi Harsharan Kaur avoided the guards and arrived at the Fort.

She saw that bodies were lying everywhere and distinguishing between Sikh and Mughal was very difficult. She still had faith and began to find arms with Karas and torsos with kachheras and heads with long Kesh. As she found a body, she would wipe the face of every Shaheed. Both Sahibzadas and about 30 Shaheeds were found and then she began to collect wood. Fearing the approaching light of dawn, Bibi Harsharan Kaur worked very quickly and soon prepared a pyre. She then lit the fire.

Seeing the rising flames, the guards were shocked and advanced towards the pyre. Bibi Harsharan Kaur was seen in the light of the flames sitting beside the pyre. She was quietly reciting Kirtan Sohila (a prayer read for cremations). The guards were shocked and confused as to how a lone woman could come into the fort on such a dark night.

The guards asked in a loud voice: *Who are you?*

Bibi Jee: *I am the daughter of Guru Gobind Singh*

Officer: *What are you doing here?*

Bibi Jee: *I am cremating my martyred brothers.*

Officer: *Don't you know about the order that coming here is a crime?*

Bibi Jee: *I know it.*

Officer: *Then why have you disobeyed that order?*

Bibi Jee: *The orders of a false king (Aurangzeb) do not stand before the orders of the Sachay Patshah (True King, Sri Guru Gobind Singh Jee)*

Officer: *Meaning?*

Bibi Jee: *Meaning that I have respect for the Singhs in my heart and with the Guru's grace I have done my duty. I don't care about your King's orders.*

Hearing such stern answers from Bibi Harsharan Kaur, the infuriated Mughal Soldiers attempted to capture her and attack. Bibi Jee grabbed her Kirpan and fought back with determination. After killing and maiming many soldiers, Bibi Harsharan Kaur was injured and fell to the ground. The soldiers picked Bibi Harsharan Kaur up and threw her into the pyre, burning her alive.

The next day the cordon around the Fort was lifted because it was clear that the Sahibzade and most of the Shaheed Singhs had been cremated. The ancestors of the Phulkiaan family, Rama and Triloka, then cremated the remaining Singhs. The story of Bibi Harsharan Kaur reached Sri Guru Gobind Singh Jee Maharaj in Talvandee Sabo (Damdama Sahib).

Upon hearing of her daughter's martyrdom, the old mother thanked Akaal Purakh (Immortal Lord). She said, "My daughter has proven herself worthy."

The story of the cremation of the Chamkaur Shaheeds will forever serve as a glowing star of inspiration for all Singhs and Singhnees." (Adapted from Mahinder Singh ChachraaRee in Soora December 1997, Translated by Admin www.tapoban.org)

What happened that you have
killed four children (my sons);
the coiled snake
(in the form of my Khalsa) still remains.
What manliness you have shown by
extinguishing a few sparks (Sahibzadas).
You have made the conflagration
brighter and more furious.
(Zafarnama, Sri Dasam Granth)

18 SHAHEEDI OF YOUNGER SAHIBZADE

After being separated from their family at the River Sirsa – Mata Gujari Jee, Sahibzada Baba Zoravar Singh Jee & Sahibzada Baba Fateh Singh Jee were double-crossed by Gangu Brahmin who had taken them in. He got greedy and wanted to steal some of the wealth that Mata Gujari Jee had upon her and he informed on them getting them subsequently arrested by the Mughals which led to their Shaheedi (martyrdom). The Sahibzade were 7 and 9 years old and were the younger sons of Sri Guru Gobind Singh Jee.

Sahibzada Baba Fateh Singh Jee is famous for being one of the first Nihang Singhs (warriors). He had dressed in full battle attire and approached Sri Guru Gobind Singh Jee and said he can also enter battle, much like his elder brothers. It was this indomitable spirit of this 7 year old which today inspires many a Sikh warrior. Guru Jee had been very pleased with his youngest son for showing this valour and spirit and granted boons that Sikh warriors for generations would take his example of high spirits as an inspiration to live by.

After being arrested the Sahibzade were bought to the court of the Governor of Sirhind - Wazir Khan, on a number of occasions, where they were offered bribes and enticements to relinquish their faith. The Sahibzade flatly refused the bribes.

An order was given to brick them alive after all attempts to convert them to Islam had failed. They bravely underwent the torture of being bricked alive and the wall that was being built around them, kept on collapsing. The executioners then stabbed the Sahibzade in order to murder them. Their martyrdom reverberates around the world and inspires us all.

Mata Gujari Jee upon hearing of the Shaheedi (martyrdom) of her younger grandsons decided to leave her body and also ascended to Sachkand (the highest spiritual dimension). She left her body at will via meditation.

19 MACHIVARA

When leaving Chamkaur – Sri Guru Gobind Singh Jee had said to Pyare Bhai Deya Singh Jee that if they get separated then they should follow a certain star (in the sky) which will lead them back to Guru Jee. In the darkness of the night and confusion of fighting off the opposing forces the Singhs did get separated from Guru Jee.

Guru Jee made it to Machiwara and to the garden of a Sikh named Gulaba. Guru Sahib took rest under a tree after fighting for days and not resting at all. Pyare Bhai Deya Singh Jee, Pyare Bhai Dharam Singh Jee and Bhai Maan Singh Jee after following the star as advised by Guru Sahib found Guru Jee asleep under the tree. When the Sikhs approached the Guru and bowed at his feet – he immediately drew his sword as he was still battle ready. He had to stop short of taking the head off of Bhai Deya Singh. It was here that Guru Jee uttered the following Shabad – which showed their untainted love for Akaal Purakh (the timeless Lord),

THOUGHT OF THE TENTH KING

Convey to the dear friend (God) the condition of the disciples, Without Thee, taking cover with a quilt is like a disease and living in a house is like living with serpents. The flask is like the spike, the cup is like a dagger and (the separation of God) is like enduring the knife of butchers. The pallet (straw mattress) of the beloved Friend (God) is most pleasing and the worldly pleasures are like a furnace. (Dasam Granth, 1347)

The Guru and the Sikhs then had to quickly recover and move on. The Gurus' waistband (kamarkassa) had not been removed for days due to the constant engagement of battle and was bloodied and stuck. It had to be removed with warm water and much tender approach. The Guru had many blisters upon his feet, his clothes were tethered and he had lost his sons and most close followers in the last few days – yet he remained undeterred and maintained a positive outlook.

20 SRI GURU GRANTH SAHIB JEE

From Machivara the Guru and a few Sikhs travelled through Punjab and another battle ensued at what is now called Muktsar Sahib. From there on, the Guru never engaged in battle again, although they remained battle ready. They settled at Sabo Ki Talwandi and what is now referred to as Takhat Sri Damdama Sahib.

An earlier occurrence at Anandpur Sahib was to shape what would take place at Damdama Sahib. A Sikh who would complete his daily prayer of the Panj Granthi (a collection of prayers from Sri Guru Granth Sahib Jee) with love and respect made a pronunciation error whilst reading. The Sikh was made to realise that Gurbani (the Gurus' scripture) is an ang (limb) of Guru Jee and making a mistake while reciting Gurbani is like hurting Guru Jee. Following this, Pyare Bhai Deya Singh along with other respected Sikhs requested the Guru to teach them the correct pronunciations of Gurbani, 'Oh keeper of the poor! Bless us with the understanding of Gurbani. Without an understanding we don't whether what we do is correct or incorrect.'

The Guru would never refuse the request of a Sikh. Thus, now settled at Damdama Sahib, the Guru gave the following command to his Gursikhs. "Go to Dhir Mal (he was the elder brother of Sri Guru Har Rai Sahib Jee) who is at Kartarpur Sahib. Sri Guru Arjan Dev Sahib Jee who compiled the Aad Granth had left room for the inclusion of the ninth Gurus' Gurbani. I will do as you request and bless you with the understanding of Gurbani."

Shaheed Baba Deep Singh Jee along with 24 other Singhs were turned away by Dhir Mal with the following message. "If your Guru is the same roop (form) as the first and fifth Kings, then why doesn't he fashion Gurbani from memory?" Dhir Mal was opposed to the Guru and had set himself up as a Guru too, hence the rebuttal.

Guru Jee answered this taunt of Dhir Mal in the following way. Shaheed Bhai Mani Singh Jee scribed as Guru Sahib Jee compiled Sri Guru Granth Sahib Jee from his sacred tongue (from memory). There were such great blessings that Jap(u) Jee Sahib, Rehraas Sahib and Kirtan Sohila were written on the first morning. On that evening the Sikh congregation listened to the meanings of the completed Gurbani. The understanding of the Gurbani that was written at amrit vela (ambrosial hours of the morning) would be explained in the evening to the congregation. Shaheed Baba Deep Singh Jee with firm faith would complete the seva (voluntary service) of providing the paper, pens and ink.

In this way within 9 months and 9 days, on the full moon of Katak, Samat 1762, till until 1763 Bikrami 23 Savan, the understanding of Gurbani was taught. With the inclusion of the ninth Gurus' Bani, Sri Guru Granth Sahib Jee was completed. A great benevolence was done to the world.

After seeing and listening to this limitless, powerful knowledge, the congregation as well the atheists were astonished. By listening to Guru Sahib Jee, the congregation of Damdama Sahib were given the opportunity to rectify their lives. There were 48 Singhs who listened to the whole recital of Sri Guru Granth Sahib Jee, they gained Brahm Gian (the wisdom of God) and were liberated whilst alive. This knowledge has been passed down the generations through the 'Giania dee Sampardai' translated as the 'school of scholars', which is now commonly referred to as Damdami Taksal. (source: www.damdamitaksal.com)

21 HAZUR SAHIB, NANDED

After completing the writing of Sri Guru Granth Sahib Jee, the Guru and his most devout Sikhs travelled south and settled in what is now the city of Nanded. It was here that the Guru would spend his final days and anoint Sri Guru Granth Sahib Jee as the eternal spiritual Guru of the Sikhs and anoint Panj Pyare – or five Sikhs of resolute discipline as the physical Guru of the Sikhs.

At Nanded, Sri Guru Gobind Singh Jee taught the meanings and correct pronunciations of all the Gurbani of Sri Dasam Granth. This took place mostly at what is now called Naghina Ghat Gurdwara in Nanded. These teachings have also been passed down the generations and many Sikhs go and live at Hazur Sahib to gain this knowledge.

Sri Guru Gobind Singh Jee was attacked by two assassins in 1708, who were deputed by Wazir Khan of Sirhind – who feared the friendship of Guru Jee with Bahadur Shah the Mughal ruler at the time. Guru Jee was stabbed and wounded. Guru Sahib killed one assassin by immediately drawing his sword – whilst the other ran out to escape – he was killed by the Sikhs whilst he tried to flee the scene. Guru Sahib's wound was treated and stitched but the stitches came out again when Guru Jee tried out a new bow. Guru Sahib then decided to not treat the wound again and said it is time for him to depart from the world.

Guru Sahib bowed to Sri Guru Granth Sahib Jee in the presence of Panj Pyare at Takhat Sri Hazur Sahib, this took place at the big Nishan Sahib which is just before the final steps leading to Takhat Sahib. Guru Sahib said the eternal Guru is now Sri Guru Granth Sahib Jee and the physical form of the Guru is represented in Panj Pyare. So from this point on to the present day Sikhs get spiritual solace and guidance from Sri Guru Granth Sahib Jee. They can get other doubts dispelled or issues addressed by approaching 'Panj Pyare' – five Sikhs of very good discipline, ideally at an initiation ceremony – Amrit Sanchar.

22 CONCLUDING REMARKS

Sri Guru Gobind Singh Jee – completed the mission of the ten Sikh Gurus by creating the Khalsa and anointing Sri Guru Granth Sahib Jee as the eternal Guru of the Sikhs. He miraculously achieved so much in a short life span of 42 years.

This short biography does not do his history justice and is a mere snapshot of his life and times. Those wishing to read further should read Dr Bhai Vir Singhs' 'Kalghidhar Chamatkar' and read or listen to 'Sooraj Parkash' by Bhai Santokh Singh Jee. These sources need to be visited to get a more in-depth knowledge, whilst they were written many years after the Gurus' life they do give us valuable insights overall. As with any source of information, we may not agree with everything they write but reading them is a must.

This book was written to draw together research I had conducted in compiling posts for social media for Akaal Publishers which had coincided with the 350th birth anniversary celebrations of Sri Guru Gobind Singh Jee at Patna Sahib. I wanted to centralize the research into one resource so it was not lost – hence why this book came into being.

I hope the book is a source of inspiration and induces readers to study and research Sri Guru Gobind Singh more. Sorry for any mistakes in compiling the book. I look forward to feedback and producing future editions of the book.

BIBLIOGRAPHY & SOURCES USED

1. **www.thesikhencyclopedia.com**

2. **www.sikhitothemax.com**

3. **www.searchgurbani.com**

4. 'Kalghidar Chamatkar' Bhai Vir Singh

5. 'Sooraj Parkash' Bhai Santokh singh

6. **www.tapoban.org**

7. Vaiksahi booklet - **www.akaalpublishers.com**

8. 'Sikh code of conduct' translated by Harjinder Singh

9. **www.damdamitaksal.com**

Made in the USA
Middletown, DE
07 August 2023

36301381R00033